T0381342

Godly wisdom from a mother to her son

(A coming of age conversation from a mother's heart To her son's ears)

"Put on the Whole Armour of God Son"

Written by Mrs. Lisa Hayes Johnson
Inspire by Mr. Brandon Darren Sapp
Editor Ms. Jo Hamilton

To order additional copies of this book, contact:
Xlibris
844-714-8691
www.Xlibris.com
Orders@Xlibris.com

ISBN: Softcover   978-1-4500-4321-2
           EBook   979-8-3694-0713-4

Print information available on the last page

Rev. date: 09/08/2023

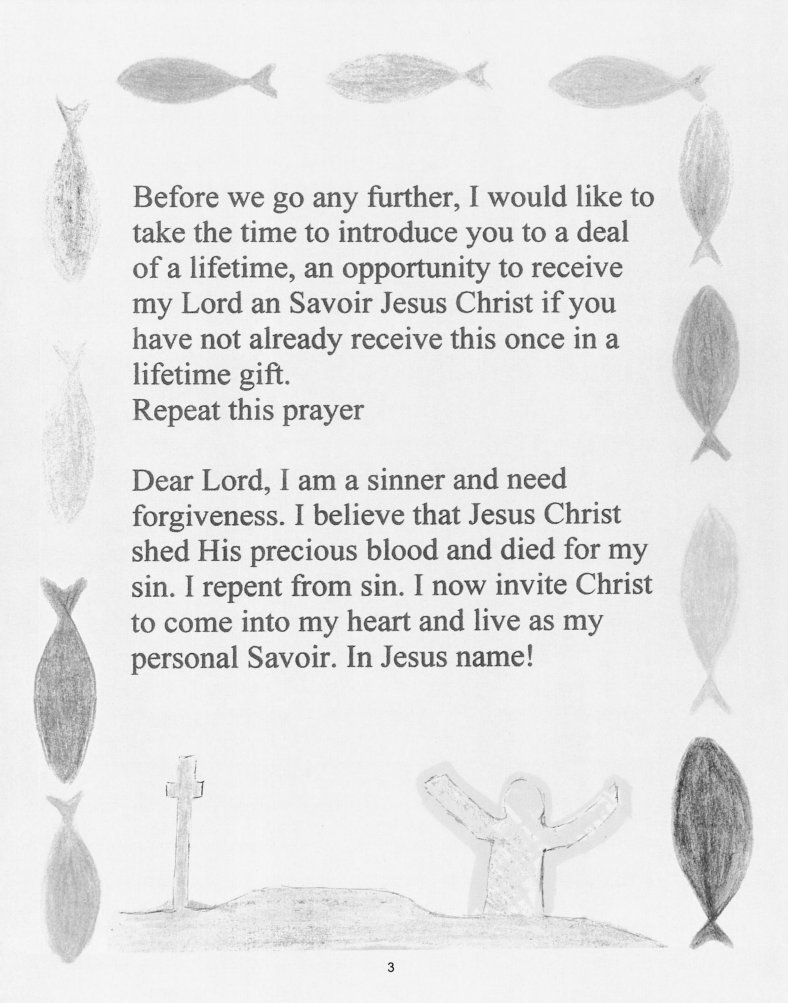

Before we go any further, I would like to take the time to introduce you to a deal of a lifetime, an opportunity to receive my Lord an Savoir Jesus Christ if you have not already receive this once in a lifetime gift.
Repeat this prayer

Dear Lord, I am a sinner and need forgiveness. I believe that Jesus Christ shed His precious blood and died for my sin. I repent from sin. I now invite Christ to come into my heart and live as my personal Savoir. In Jesus name!

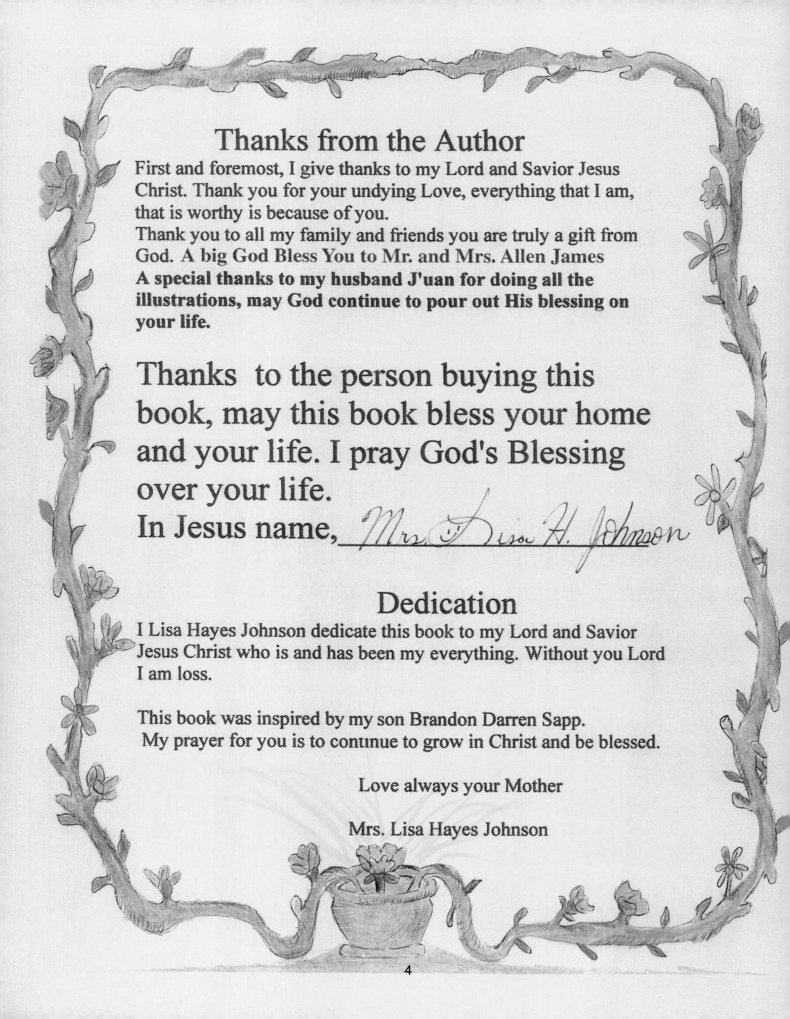

Thanks from the Author

First and foremost, I give thanks to my Lord and Savior Jesus Christ. Thank you for your undying Love, everything that I am, that is worthy is because of you.

Thank you to all my family and friends you are truly a gift from God. A big God Bless You to Mr. and Mrs. Allen James

A special thanks to my husband J'uan for doing all the illustrations, may God continue to pour out His blessing on your life.

Thanks to the person buying this book, may this book bless your home and your life. I pray God's Blessing over your life. In Jesus name,_____

Dedication

I Lisa Hayes Johnson dedicate this book to my Lord and Savior Jesus Christ who is and has been my everything. Without you Lord I am loss.

This book was inspired by my son Brandon Darren Sapp. My prayer for you is to continue to grow in Christ and be blessed.

Love always your Mother

Mrs. Lisa Hayes Johnson

4

THIS BOOK IS PRESENTED TO

_____

BY

_____

ON

DATE _____

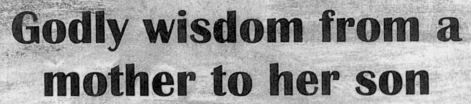

Godly wisdom from a mother to her son

(A coming of age conversation from a mother's heart To her son's ears)

"Put on the Whole Armour of God Son"

Written by Mrs. Lisa Hayes Johnson
Inspire by Mr. Brandon Darren Sapp
Editor Ms. Jo Hamilton

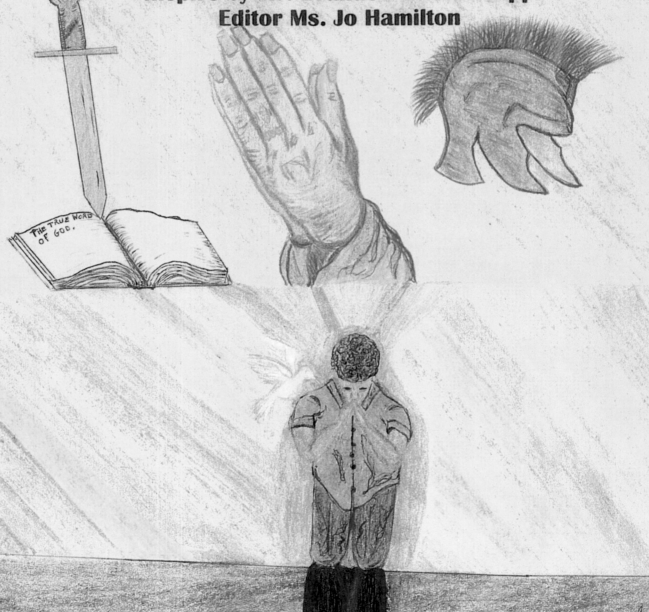

THE TRUE WORD OF GOD.

Dear_____ (Mighty Young man of God)

I pray that this book reaches you in the best of physical and spiritual health, and may your soul prosper as your life prospers. The reason and purpose I am writing you is because you will soon come of age.
I am taking this time to welcome you to manhood.
When you were born, I had no idea what a blessing it would be to be your parent.
Son, you are one of the greatest and best things that have ever happen to me.
You were only given to your father and I for a season, to groom and teach you
God's precepts;
It is our duty to the Lord Jesus Christ and to you to do the best we can to show you Christ, who died so that we might be free. You came from God. The Bible states before you entered into my wound, God knew you.

(Isiah 44:2)

This Book is dedicated to you becoming a man of God!

7

It has been, and is, wonderful, hard, heartbreaking, delightful and a pure Joy being your mother.

Being a parent is the hardest, but the most rewarding job, a person will ever be blessed with.

When you were born, it was an overwhelming moment in my life.

I didn't have any idea how we were going to raise you or even take care of ourselves, but God made a way for your father and I.

It is an honor and a pleasure to be your mother.

Remember you have gifts given to you from God. Do not forget to practice and work hard to use these gifts to be a blessing to God's Kingdom and yourself.

Son, once again, I want to state the fact that it has and is (I will always be mama) a privilege being your mother. As a mother, I will share with you some solutions to survive and thrive in this life.

Take this wisdom from my heart to Yours!

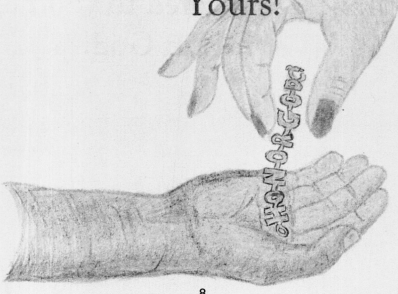

Be strong in the Lord, and in the power of his might. Put on the whole armour of God, that you may be able to stand against the wiles of the devil.

For we wrestle not against flesh and blood, but against principalities, against powers, against the rulers of the darkness of this world, against spiritual wickedness in high places.

Wherefore take unto you the whole armour of God, that you may be able to withstand in the evil day, and having done all, to stand.

{ EPHESIANS } CH. 6

Take the helmet of Salvation

Having on the Breastplate of Righteousness

Therefore, having your loins girt about with truth,

Taking the Shield of faith, Wherewith you shall be able to quench all the fiery darts of the wicked.

Your feet Shod with the Preparation of the gospel of peace

The Sword of the Spirit, which is the word of God.

Drawn by Mr. J-vax John

12-05

9

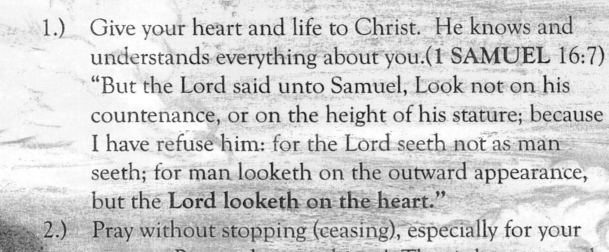

1.) Give your heart and life to Christ. He knows and understands everything about you.(**1 SAMUEL** 16:7) "But the Lord said unto Samuel, Look not on his countenance, or on the height of his stature; because I have refuse him: for the Lord seeth not as man seeth; for man looketh on the outward appearance, but the **Lord looketh on the heart.**"

2.) Pray without stopping (ceasing), especially for your enemy. Prayer changes things! That is how we made it this far. (**NUMBERS** 10:35) "And it came to pass, when the ark set forward, that Moses said, Rise up, Lord, and let thine enemies be scattered; and let them that hate thee flee before thee."
    (**PSALM** 55: 16-19) "16. As for me, I will call upon God; and the Lord shall save me. 17. Evening, and morning, and at noon, will I pray, and cry aloud: and he shall hear my voice. 18. He hath delivered my soul in peace from the battle that was against me: for there were many with me. 19. God shall hear, and afflict them, even he that abideth of old. Selah. Because they have no changes, therefore they fear not God."

3.) Remember there is nothing too hard for God, but God gives us free will. If we do not choose His will, we will regret it. (II CORINTHIANS 1:2-5)

4.) "2. Grace be to you and peace from God our Father, and from the Lord Jesus Christ. 3. Blessed be God, even the Farther of our Lord Jesus Christ, the Father of mercies, and the God of all comfort; 4. Who comforteth us in all our tribulation, that we may be able to comfort them which are in any trouble, by the comfort wherewith we ourselves are comforted of God. 5. For as the sufferings of Christ abound in us, so our consolation also aboundeth by Christ.

5.) Keep yourself Holy as unto the Lord, and if you do not, repent! For the Kingdom of Heaven is at hand, so get it right with God. God is a forgiving God, full of grace and mercy. He has forgiven me so many times, but we must pay for what we do. You reap what you sow."(ROMANS 12:1-2)1.I beseech you therefore, brethren, by the mercies of God, that ye present your bodies a living sacrifice, holy, acceptable unto God, which is your reasonable service.2. And be not conformed to this world: but be ye transformed by the renewing of your mind, that ye may prove what is that good, and accepted, and perfect, will of God."

6.) Pay your tithes! Remember, God doesn't need your money, but you need His blessings. This is how God kept a roof over our heads. I trusted God and paid my tithes and offerings. This is such a small thing to do for God, who does so much for us. Do not ever let the love of money come between you and God. "Where your heart is, there also is your treasure." Ten percent goes straight to God.

(MALACHI 3:8-12) 8. "Will a man rob God? Yet ye have robbed me. But ye say wherein have we robbed thee? In tithes and offerings. 9. Ye are curse with a curse: for ye have robbed me, even this whole nation. 10. Bring ye all the tithes into the storehouse, that there may be meat in mine house, and prove me now herewith, saith the Lord of hosts, if I will not open you the windows of heaven, and pour you out a blessing, that there shall not be room enough to receive it. 11. And I will rebuke the devourer for your sakes, and he shall not destroy the fruits of your ground; neither shall your vine cast her fruit before the time in the field, saith the Lord of hosts. 12. And all nations shall call you blessed: for ye shall be a delightsome land, saith the Lord of hosts"

7.) Acknowledge what you learned from your father and mother. Remember and use the good, but throw away the bad. (**EXODUS** 2:2) "And the woman conceived, and bare a son: and when she saw him that he was a goodly child, she hid him three months."(**PROVERBS** 3:11-13) "My son, despise not the chastening of the Lord; neither be weary of his correction: 12. For whom the Lord loveth he correcteth; even as a father the son in whom he delighteth. 13. Happy is the man that findeth wisdom, and the man that getteth understanding."

8.) Guard your eyes and ears. It is so important that you be careful of what you watch and hear. If you watch violence, you will have more violent thoughts. "Evil communication corrupts good manners." Meditate on good and pure things. (**PHILIPPIANS** 4:8-9) "Finally, brethren, whatsoever things are true, whatsoever things are honest, whatsoever things are just, whatsoever are pure, whatsoever things are lovely, whatsoever things are of good report; if there be any virtue, and if there be any praise, think on these things.9. Those things, which ye have both learned, and received, and heard, and seen in me, do: and the God of peace shall be with you.) This will take you far in life."

9.) Give back to others; it is a blessing to give. Not because they deserve it, but because Jesus has given so much to us and for us. He is the gift that keeps on giving. Look at the many things He has given us which we do not deserve. (JOHN 3:16-17) "For God so loved the world that he gave his only begotten Son, that whosoever believeth in him should not perish, but have everlasting life.17. For God sent not his Son into the world to condemn the world; but that the world through him might be saved."

10.) Guard your heart; pray (**PSALM** 51:10-15). "10. Create in me a clean heart, O God; and renew a right spirit within me. 11. Cast me not away from thy presence; and take not thy holy spirit from me.12. Restore unto me the joy of thy salvation; and uphold me with thy free spirit.13. Then will I teach transgressors thy ways; and sinners shall be converted unto thee.14. Deliver me from blood guiltiness, O God, thou God of my salvation: and my tongue shall sing aloud of thy righteousness.15. O Lord, open thou my lips; and my mouth shall shew forth thy praise."

11.) Do not entrust your heart to anyone unless they love the Lord and walk with integrity. (**PROVERBS** 11:3) "The integrity of the upright shall guide them: but the perverseness of transgressors shall destroy them."

12.) Pray for the women that come into your life. Most are there to get you closer to God one way or another, whether they are evil or of God.

(1 **THESSALONIANS** 4:3-6) "3. For this is the will of God, even your sanctification, that ye should abstain from fornication: 4. That every one of you should know how to possess his vessel in sanctification and honour; 5. Not in the lust of concupiscence, even as Gentiles which know not God: 6. That no man go beyond and defraud his brother in any matter: because that the Lord is the avenger of all such, as we also have forewarned you and testified."

13.) Always treat a lady with respect and Godly love. If you cannot respect her, you do not need her. Move on, life is too short to waste it. (**I PETER** 2:17) "Honour all men. Love the brotherhood. Fear God. Honour the king."

14.) Never fall for a woman who chases after you. Remember that you are the man and the hunter. If you do not fight to get her, you will not fight to keep her. Your wife should be God's and your choice. (**PROVERBS** 18:22) "Whoso findeth a wife findeth a good thing, and obtaineth favour of the Lord."

15.) Always work hard, and give your best. In the end God will reward you. (**PROVERBS** 14:23) "In all labour there is profit: but the talk of the lips tendeth only to penury."

16.) Don't lie! It is not healthy, and it will stop you from getting some special blessings God has for you. (**PROVERBS** 12:19-22) "19. The lip of truth shall be established for ever: but a lying tongue is but for a moment. 20. Deceit is in the heart of them that imagine evil: but to the counselors of peace is joy. 21. There shall no evil happen to the just: but the wicked shall be filled with mischief. 22. Lying lips are abomination to the Lord: but they that deal truly are his delight."

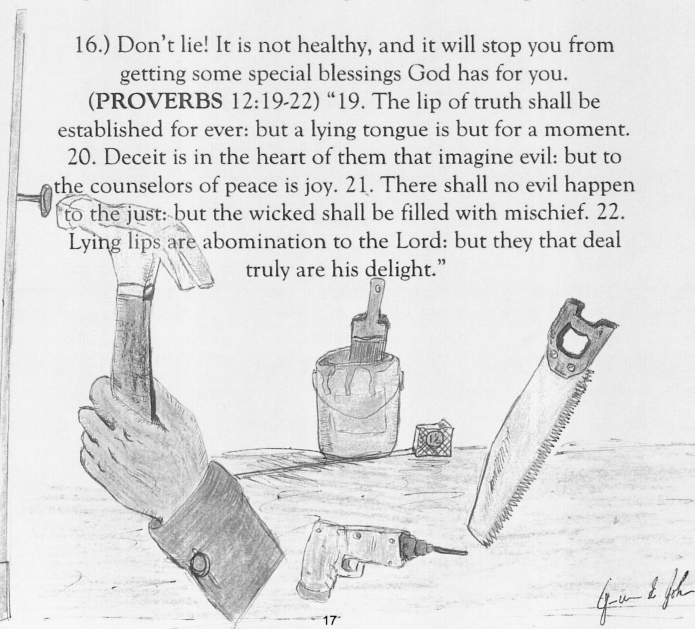

17.) Don't take life for granted. Enjoy every moment. Jesus died so that you may live. A lot of your ancestors died for you to have the freedom and the rights you have. Honor them with respect. (**I SAMUEL** 2:1) "And Hannah prayed, and said, my heart rejoiceth in the Lord, mine horn is exalted in the Lord; my mouth is enlarged over mine enemies; because I rejoice in thy salvation."

18.) Learn whatever you can about the Bible. The word of God adds wisdom and changes lives. (**NUMBERS** 23:19) "God is not a man, that he should lie; neither the son of man, that he should repent: hath he said, and shall he not do it? Or hath he spoken, and shall he not make it good?"

19.) When you get married, pray over your wife and children. Live Holy, and your children and wife will follow your lead. Swallow your pride and do what is right as unto the Lord. Do not let days go by without Hugging and Kissing them, for God is love. (**JOSHUA** 3:5) "And Joshua said unto the people, Sanctify yourselves: for tomorrow the Lord will do wonders among you."(**ROMANS** 16:16) "Salute one another with an holy kiss. The churches of Christ salute you."

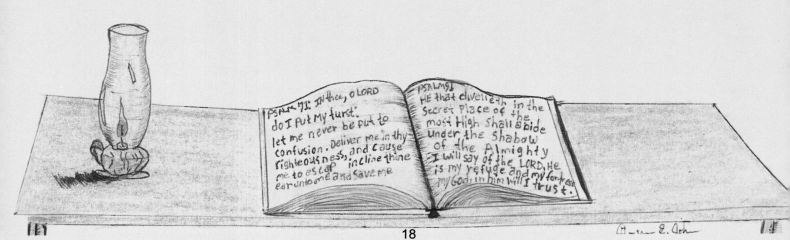

20.) Remember you were created to worship God. When praises go up, blessing comes down. Do not ever be afraid to worship and pray. There is nothing more powerful than a praising and praying man. **(PSALMS** 29:1-2) "Give unto the Lord, O ye mighty, give unto the Lord Glory and strength. 2. Give unto the Lord the glory due unto his name; worship the Lord in the beauty of holiness."

21.) Learn to cook and clean. Healthy meals will keep you around longer and save you money. Choose life, this world needs you. Go for walks as often as you can, and take this time to think and talk with God. These walks will breathe new life into you. **(ROMANS** 12:1) "I BESEECH you therefore, brethren, by the mercies of God, that ye present your bodies a living sacrifice holy, acceptable unto God, which is your reasonable service."

22.) Stand up for righteousness! Stand behind the word of God for it is a light unto your feet.

23.) Never lean to your own understanding. Before you make decisions, seek God's face. If you follow His advice, you will be blessed beyond your dreams. **(PROVERBS** 3:5) "Trust in the Lord with all thine heart; and lean not unto thine own understanding."

24.) Whenever you are in trouble, call on Jesus. There is no other name that causes demons to flee and every knee to bow. Your help comes from the Lord. **(PSALMS** 91) "1. He that dwelleth in the secret place of the most High shall abide under the shadow of the Almighty. 2. I will say of the Lord, He is my refuge and my fortress: my God; in him will I trust. 3. Surely he shall deliver thee from the snare of the fowler, and from the noisome pestilence. 4. He shall cover thee with his feathers, and under his wings shalt thou trust: his truth shall be thy shield and buckler. 5. Thou shalt not be afraid for the terror by night: nor for the arrow that flieth by day; 6. Nor for the pestilence that walketh in darkness; nor for the destruction that wasteth at noonday. 7. A thousand shall fall at thy side, and ten thousand at thy right hand; but it shall not come nigh thee. 8. Only with thine eyes shalt thou behold and see the reward of the wicked. 9. Because thou hast made the Lord, which is my refuge, even the most High, thy habitation; 10. There shall no evil befall thee, neither shall any plague come nigh thy dwelling. 11. For he shall give his angels charge over thee, to keep thee in all thy ways. 12. They shall bear thee up in their hands, lest thou dash thy foot against a stone. 13. Thou shalt tread upon the lion and adder: the young lion and the dragon shalt thou trample under feet. 14. Because he hath set his love upon me, therefore will I deliver him: I will set him on high, because he hath known my name. 15. He shall call upon me, and I will answer him: I will be with him in trouble; I will deliver him, and honour him. 16. With long life will I satisfy him and shew him my salvation."

25.) In everything give thanks, for it is the will of God for your life. God loves a thankful heart.

(1 **THESSALONIANSON** 5:16-24) "Rejoice evermore. 17. Pray without ceasing. 18. In every thing give thanks: for this is the will of God in Christ Jesus concerning you. 19. Quench not the spirit. 20. Despise not prophesyings. 21. Prove all things; hold fast that which is good. 22. Abstain from all appearance of evil. 23. And the very God of peace sanctify you wholly; and I pray God your whole spirit and soul and body be preserved blameless unto the coming of our Lord Jesus Christ.24. Faithful is he that calleth you, who also will do it."

26.) Laugh a lot it will make and keep you healthy. (**PROVERBS** 17:22) "A merry heart doeth good like a medicine: but a broken spirit drieth the bones."

27.) Cry whenever it is needed. Strong men cry. It is a part of the healing process. Jesus did.

28.) Read the book of John for it will teach you about love. (**JOHN** 15:12) "This is my commandment, That ye love one another, as I have loved you."

29.) Always love and pray for your family in Jesus name. It may not be easy, but you need familiar spirits broken over your family. Some things only come through prayer and fasting, For God is love. (**1 THESSALONIANS** 3:12-13) "And the Lord make you to increase and abound in love one toward another, and toward all men, even as we do toward you: 13. To the end he may stablish your hearts unblameable in holiness before God, even our Farther, at the coming of our Lord Jesus Christ with all his saints."

30.) Save money for a rainy day. Learn to invest. Stay away from credit cards as much as possible. If you get one, keep the balance low and read the small print.

31.) All good things come from God. He is the beginning and the end, the Alpha and Omega. Do what God says and leave the consequences to Him.

32.) Stand still, Live holy and know that God will show up! (**EPHESIANS** 5:8) "For ye were sometimes darkness, but now are ye light in the Lord: walk as children of light:"

BIBLE VERSES FROM THE KING JAMES BIBLE

GOD LOVES YOU SO MUCH THAT, HE ALWAYS SENDS HIS WORD!
BE BLESS.

Be glad then, ye children of Zion   Joel.2:23
But it is good for me to draw near to God
Ps.73:28
And now abideth faith, hope, charity, these three
1Cor.13:13
But he that built all things is God   Heb.3:4
That which I see not teach thou me   Job.34:32
The LORD is good unto them that wait for him
Lam.3:25
It shall be well with them that fear God
Eccl.8:12
Thanks be unto God for his unspeakable gift
2Cor.9:15
But thanks be to God, which giveth us the victory
1Cor.15:57
Prosper, I pray thee, thy servant this day
Neh.1:11
Blessed be the Lord... daily   Ps.68:19
I will bless thee... and thou shalt be a blessing
Gen.12:2
He will bless them that fear the LORD   Ps.115:13
Blessed is the man that endureth temptation
James.1:12
Blessed is..., whose sin is covered   Ps.32:1
Blessed are ye that weep now: for ye shall laugh
Luke.6:21
The word is nigh thee, even in thy mouth, and in thy
heart   Rom.10:8
But the end of all things is at hand   1Pet.4:7
God was in Christ, reconciling the world unto
himself 2Cor.5:19
God hath given to us eternal life   1John.5:11
For God is love 1John.4:8
God is light, and in him is no darkness at all
1John.1:5
And God is able to make all grace abound toward you
2Cor.9:8

But my God shall supply all your need   Phil.4:19
God is a refuge for us   Ps.62:8
Our God whom we serve is able to deliver us
Dan.3:17
For it is God which worketh in you both to will and
to do of his good pleasure   Phil.2:13
I am the LORD thy God which teacheth thee to profit
Is.48:17
Where is God my maker, who giveth songs in the night
Job.35:10
Now the God of patience and consolation Rom.15:5
Watch and pray   Matt.26:41
Watch ye, stand fast in the faith   1Cor.16:13
Keep thy heart with all diligence   Prov.4:23
I will remember thy wonders of old   Ps.77:11
Yea, I will rejoice over them to do them good
Jer.32:41
There shall be showers of blessing   Ezek.34:26
Be thou faithful unto death, and I will give thee a
crown of life   Rev.2:10
Be kindly affectioned one to another with brotherly
love   Rom.12:10
Be of one mind, live in peace   2Cor.13:11
But be ye doers of the word   James.1:22
So be ye holy in all manner of conversation
1Pet.1:15
Be ye holy; for I am holy   1Pet.1:16
To be ready to every good work   Titus.3:1
Receive with meekness the engrafted word
James.1:21
That in every thing ye are enriched by him
1Cor.1:5
Hide me under the shadow of thy wings   Ps.17:8
Great peace have they which love thy law
Ps.119:165
Whereby are given unto us exceeding great and
precious promises   2Pet.1:4
Faith without works is dead...   James.2:26

So then faith cometh by hearing, and hearing by the
word of God   Rom.10:17
Believe ye that I am able to do this?   Matt.9:28
He that believeth on him shall not be confounded
1Pet.2:6
Everlasting joy shall be unto them   Is.61:7
And thou shalt rejoice before the LORD thy God
Deut.12:18
Seek ye me, and ye shall live   Amos.5:4
For the things which are seen are temporal; but the
things which are not seen are eternal   2Cor.4:18
Draw me, we will run after thee Song.1:4
I all their affliction he was afflicted, and the
angel of his presence saved them   Is.63:9
Lift up your hands... and bless the LORD
Ps.134:2
Call unto me, and I will answer thee   Jer.33:3
I will cry unto God... that performeth all things
for me   Ps.57:2
Cast thy burden upon the LORD   Ps.55:22
Beloved, now are we the sons of God   1John.3:2
But grow in grace   2Pet.3:18
God... hath begotten us ... To an inheritance
incorruptible, and undefiled   1Pet.1:3,4
And take up his cross daily, and follow me
Luke.9:23
I will go in the strength of the Lord GOD
Ps.71:16
Will of God is good, and acceptable, and perfect
Rom.12:2
Of his own will begat he us with the word of truth
James.1:18
Behold, now is the day of salvation   2Cor.6:2
For ye are all one in Christ Jesus   Gal.3:28
Do all to the glory of God   1Cor.10:31
Casting all your care upon him 1Pet.5:7
And all mine are thine, and thine are mine
John.17:10

All these things we are more than conquerors through
him that loved us   Rom.8:37
Let all your things be done with charity
1Cor.16:14
He hath done all things well   Mark.7:37
For as many as are led by the Spirit of God, they
are the sons of God   Rom.8:14
Whatsoever God doeth, it shall be for ever
Eccl.3:14
And in the morning, rising up a great while before
day…and there prayed   Mark.1:35
For whosoever shall call upon the name of the Lord
shall be saved Rom.10:13
Every good gift... is from above   James.1:17
Ye are...the epistle of Christ 2Cor.3:3
If so be ye have tasted that the Lord is gracious
1Pet.2:3
And ye are Christ's; and Christ is God's
1Cor.3:23
For ye are bought with a price 1Cor.6:20
Ye shall receive a crown of glory that fadeth not
away   1Pet.5:4
Now we have received, not the spirit of the world,
but the spirit which is of God 1Cor.2:12
But now in Christ Jesus ye... are made nigh by the
blood of Christ   Eph.2:13
And he brought forth his people with joy
Ps.105:43
Where the Spirit of the Lord is, there is liberty
2Cor.3:17
Where I am, there shall also my servant be
John.12:26
They spake the word of God with boldness
Acts.4:31
If any man speak, let him speak as the oracles of
God   1Pet.4:11
But sanctify the Lord God in your hearts
1Pet.3:15

Lord, all my desire is before thee   Ps.38:8
O LORD, revive thy work in the midst of the years
Hab.3:2
Thou shalt worship the Lord thy God   Matt.4:10
For the LORD JEHOVAH is my strength and my song
Is.12:2
The LORD will bless his people with peace
Ps.29:11
For the LORD God is a sun and shield   Ps.84:11
For in the LORD JEHOVAH is everlasting strength
Is.26:4
For the LORD shall be thine everlasting light
Is.60:20
But the LORD will be the hope of his people
Joel.3:16
That the Lord is very pitiful, and of tender mercy
James.5:11
And the LORD hath laid on him the iniquity of us all
Is.53:6
The LORD will give grace and glory   Ps.84:11
He knoweth them that trust in him   Nah.1:7
The LORD will perfect that which concerneth me
Ps.138:8
The LORD God, merciful and gracious   Ex.34:6
And I will remember their sin no more   Jer.31:34
Our God shall come, and shall not keep silence
Ps.50:3
The will of the Lord be done   Acts.21:14
Let, I pray thee, thy merciful kindness be for my
comfort Ps.119:76
Let thine hand help me   Ps.119:173
I will abide in thy tabernacle for ever Ps.61:4
We should bring forth fruit unto God   Rom.7:4
But let him ask in faith, nothing wavering
James.1:6
Let him ask of God, that giveth to all men
liberally, and upbraideth not   James.1:5
That we might receive the adoption of sons

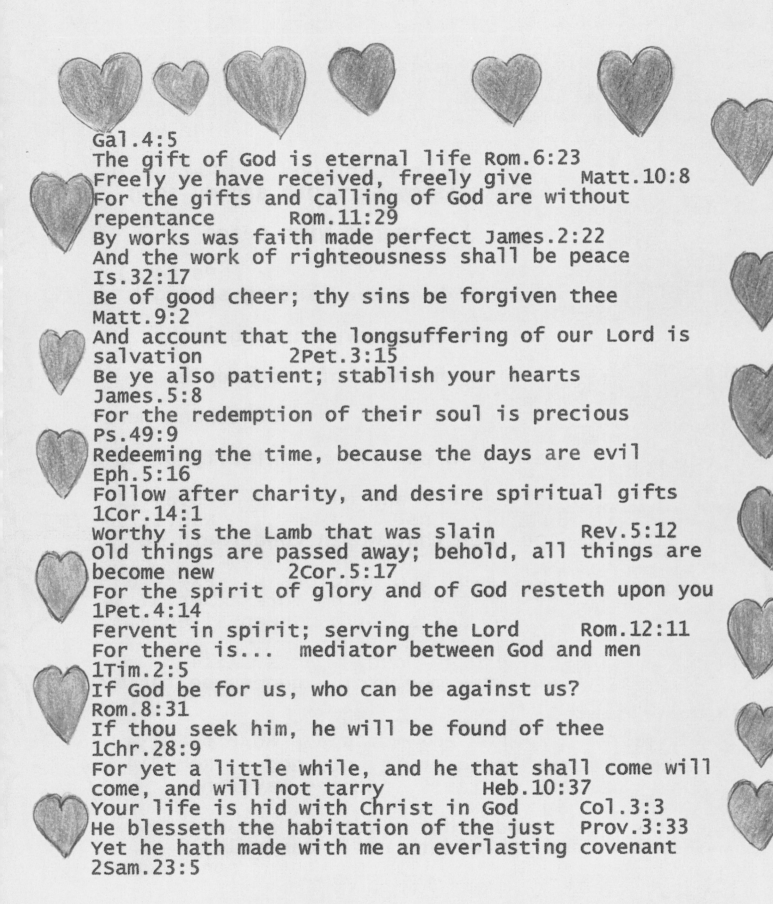

Gal.4:5
The gift of God is eternal life Rom.6:23
Freely ye have received, freely give   Matt.10:8
For the gifts and calling of God are without
repentance   Rom.11:29
By works was faith made perfect James.2:22
And the work of righteousness shall be peace
Is.32:17
Be of good cheer; thy sins be forgiven thee
Matt.9:2
And account that the longsuffering of our Lord is
salvation   2Pet.3:15
Be ye also patient; stablish your hearts
James.5:8
For the redemption of their soul is precious
Ps.49:9
Redeeming the time, because the days are evil
Eph.5:16
Follow after charity, and desire spiritual gifts
1Cor.14:1
Worthy is the Lamb that was slain   Rev.5:12
Old things are passed away; behold, all things are
become new   2Cor.5:17
For the spirit of glory and of God resteth upon you
1Pet.4:14
Fervent in spirit; serving the Lord   Rom.12:11
For there is... mediator between God and men
1Tim.2:5
If God be for us, who can be against us?
Rom.8:31
If thou seek him, he will be found of thee
1Chr.28:9
For yet a little while, and he that shall come will
come, and will not tarry   Heb.10:37
Your life is hid with Christ in God   Col.3:3
He blesseth the habitation of the just Prov.3:33
Yet he hath made with me an everlasting covenant
2Sam.23:5

Ye were sealed with that holy Spirit of promise
Eph.1:13
For the LORD knoweth the way of the righteous
Ps.1:6
For your Father knoweth what things ye have need of
Matt.6:8
Knowledge puffeth up, but charity edifieth
1Cor.8:1
And will be a Father unto you, and ye shall be my
sons and daughters   2Cor.6:18
And by him all that believe are justified from all
things Acts.13:39
Yea, they shall sing in the ways of the LORD
Ps.138:5
And I said, Thou shalt call me, My father
Jer.3:19
And a new spirit will I put within you Ezek.36:26
And the life was the light of men   John.1:4
And as many as touched him were made whole
Mark.6:56
And we have know...the love that God hath to us
1John.4:16
On earth peace, good will toward men   Luke.2:14
And to wait for his Son from heaven   1Thess.1:10
And I set my tabernacle among you   Lev.26:11
And my speech and my preaching... in demonstration
of the Spirit and of power   1Cor.2:4
And so, after Abraham had patiently endured, he
obtained the promise.   Heb.6:15
And the King shall answer and say unto them, ye have
done it unto me Matt.25:40
For the Lamb... shall feed them Rev.7:17
For the LORD taketh pleasure in his people
Ps.149:4
For the day of the LORD is at hand   Zeph.1:7
For his merciful kindness is great toward us
Ps.117:2
For, behold, I create new heavens and a new earth

Is.65:17
For all the promises of God in him are yea
2Cor.1:20
For the life was manifested   1John.1:2
For my yoke is easy, and my burden is light
Matt.11:30
For he that hath mercy on them shall lead them
Is.49:10
For we are labourers together with God 1Cor.3:9
For we are unto God a sweet savour of Christ
2Cor.2:15
For the Father himself loveth you   John.16:27
For the preaching of the cross is...the power of God
1Cor.1:18
Come, and let us join ourselves to the LORD
Jer.50:5
The word is gone out of my mouth in righteousness,
and shall not return   Is.45:23
Jesus...ever liveth to make intercession
Heb.7:22,25
Elias was a man subject to like passions as we are
James.5:17
Having therefore these promises... let us cleanse
ourselves   2Cor.7:1
The name of the LORD is a strong tower Prov.18:10
And they were all filled with the Holy Ghost
Acts.2:4
But he that doeth the will of God abideth for ever
1John.2:17
His truth endureth to all generations   Ps.100:5
Thy faithfulness reacheth unto the clouds
Ps.36:5
And now, little children, abide in him 1John.2:28
Those that seek me early shall find me Prov.8:17
My soul followeth hard after thee   Ps.63:8
O LORD, to thee will I cry   Joel.1:19
Every man shall receive his own reward according to
his own labour 1Cor.3:8